Practical Christianity

James Poole

ISBN: 978-1-78364-461-2

The Open Bible Trust
Fordland Mount, Upper Basildon,
Reading, RG8 8LU, UK.

www.obt.org.uk

Practical Christianity

Contents

Introduction

During the past years many of us have been privileged under God to receive scriptural expositions of some of the deep things of God. We have glimpsed at His glorious purpose for the ages to head up all in Christ (Ephesians 1:10), when:

> "every knee shall bow and every tongue confess that Jesus Christ is Lord to the glory of God the Father," (Philippians 2:10, 11).

We have learned that in order to understand the Scriptures they must be *rightly divided* (2 Timothy 2:15), in accordance with the particular administration, or dispensation, of God's truth in force at that time. If we apply a particular truth of one dispensation to an earlier or later one, the result may be confusion and contradiction, even error. Not only is this the case with doctrine. It is also true in practical matters.

Doctrine and Practice cannot be separated.

This is a fundamental truth that must be learned by all of us. It is the divine purpose that faith is followed by works (of faith). This is displayed through all the Scriptures but never so clearly as in Paul's epistle to the Romans. From chapter 1:1 to 6:13 he emphasizes that sheer unadulterated faith in God's testimony concerning His son's death on Calvary justifies the believer before Him.

Moreover, in grace the believer is brought into peace with God and is reckoned by God to have been dead, buried and raised with Christ. This is the unchangeable and unalterable standing of the believer before God. (See Romans 3:21-26; 5:1-2; 6:1-11). To *such* people Paul *exhorts* that they:

"yield themselves unto God as those that are alive from the dead and their members as instruments of righteousness unto Him," (Romans 6:12-13).

And, again, in Romans 12:1 Paul *beseeches* them to hand over their bodies to God,

"a living sacrifice, holy, acceptable to God, which is your reasonable service."

Here, then, is the balance between doctrine and practice, between faith and works (of faith).

There is some *gospel preaching* today which tends to put "the cart before the horse." Unsaved sinners are exhorted to "Yield to Christ!" "Let Him come into your hearts!" Unsaved sinners are told to give up this, that and the other. That is not how the greatest evangelist of all time, Paul, presented the gospel to the unsaved.

First, he proved to them by law or conscience their lost and sinful condition. Then, to convicted ones, he pointed to the Lord Jesus Christ and His sacrifice on Calvary's Cross. He told them that through faith in that sacrifice as an offering for their sins, they were justified before God. Finally, to such justified ones, to those who had the motive of love towards God and the power to please Him, to such as these, Paul exhorted a yielding of themselves and their bodies to God.

Again, in Paul's epistle to the Ephesians we have this balance between faith and works (of faith). The first three chapters are occupied with the setting forth of the wondrous, celestial calling of God which is ours in Christ Jesus. Then, in chapters four, five and six he relates this calling to the ordinary, daily affairs of life and its relationships by giving us precepts which will enable us to walk worthy of that calling.

Now if we take the precepts in Paul's epistles, apart from the doctrinal sections which precede them, and if we attempt to put them into practice, then we shall be trying to produce *fruit* without the *root* and *branch*. Any results will be artificial and unlikely to last for long, with the final state being barren.

Rightly Dividing the Word of Truth as to Practice

This is a most important principle to follow if we wish to please our Heavenly Father. Not all the practical exhortations contained in the Scriptures are applicable in this age and dispensation. Some had their true application in the past, while others will find their fulfilment in the future.

Some modern preachers and teachers talk about the Old Testament Scriptures as being cruel and barbaric – the history of primitive man. Such do not understand that under the Law which came by Moses, conduct was judged impartially and according to the righteous standards laid down. Not only in the *Ten Commandments,* but in all the statutes and ordinances which we find in the Pentateuch – the first five books of the Old Testament.

Even though the judgments were severe and terrible, they were absolutely just and often God's long-suffering, patience and loving-kindness delayed them.

Again, those who sentimentally dote about the gentleness of Jesus can forget that, in the future Millenial Kingdom upon this earth, it is not as a lamb but as the lion of Judah that He will reign, and with a rod of iron! Those of the nations on earth who will rebel against Him will be punished according to the severity of their offence.

Moreover, many of the imprecations contained in the Psalms against Israel's enemies, applicable under the Mosaic Dispensation, are quite unsuitable for use by the Church of the one Body of Christ. In this dispensation of the Grace of God, God is reconciled to all mankind and beseeches them to receive this reconciliation and be reconciled to Him. An example of an inappropriate passage is found in Psalm 137:7-9.

> Remember, O Lord, the Children of Edom in
> the day of Jerusalem; who said, "Rase it, rase

it, even to the foundation thereof." O daughter of Babylon, who art to be destroyed; happy shall he be, that rewardeth thee as thou hast served us. Happy shall he be, that taketh and dasheth thy little ones against the stones.

The spirit of this Psalm is appropriate to the dispensation of law and judgment but not to this present dispensation of grace.

Some today say that for practical Christianity we should take as our guide the teaching of the Lord Jesus recorded in the four gospels, the precepts He gave in *The Sermon on the Mount*. It is unquestionably true that many of the virtues that our Lord enumerated there, such as meekness, loving our enemies, doing good to them that hate us, know no dispensational boundaries. Paul exhorts the saints to be meek, (compare Matthew 5:5 and Ephesians 4:2).

He tells them to love their enemies, (compare Matthew 5:44 and Romans 12:20). Let us not become ultra dispensational in our handling of the four gospels and say, "There is nothing for me in them!" 2Timothy 3:16 tells us not only that all Scripture is inspired but that "All scripture is profitable for doctrine, for reproof, for correction, for instruction in righteousness."

There is much for our profit in the four gospels if we carefully "distinguish the things that differ" (Philippians 1:10 margin) in the exhortations given by Paul in his epistles and those given by our Lord recorded in the gospels.

However, it should be emphasized here that it is not a question of contrasting the precepts of Paul and Jesus Christ, but of comparing the precepts of our risen and glorified Lord, of whom Paul was just the mouthpiece, and those of our Lord in the days of His humiliation when He was incarnate in the likeness of sinful flesh. The contrast is one of degree, of the grace and truth of our Lord's words when on earth and the superabounding grace which He proclaimed from heaven. Let us take one example.

In the Lord's Prayer there is a plea to our Heavenly Father.

> Forgive us our debts, as we forgive our debtors ... For if ye forgive men their trespasses, your heavenly Father will also forgive you: but if ye forgive not men their trespasses, neither will your Father forgive your trespasses. (Matthew 6:12,14-15)

Notice that the forgiveness of trespasses is dependent on forgiving the trespasses of fellowmen. Here, indeed, is grace, but it is conditional. Now contrast this conditional grace with the exhortations given by Paul.

> Be ye kind one to another, tenderhearted, forgiving one another, even as God for Christ's sake hath forgiven you. (Ephesians 4:32)

> Forbearing one another, and forgiving one another, if any man have a quarrel against any: even as Christ forgave you, so also do ye. (Colossians 3:13)

Here is super-abounding grace. It is unconditional. It is not dependent on our forgiveness of others, and, because of this very fact, it should be a more powerful incentive for our hearts to forgive others also.

If we want to be filled with the knowledge of our heavenly Father's will, with all spiritual understanding in order that we may walk worthily of the Lord unto all pleasing, being fruitful in every good word – as Colossians 1:9-10 puts it – then we need first to be steeped in both the doctrine and practice revealed by the risen and glorified Christ which is contained in Paul's later epistles (Ephesians, Philippians, Colossians, 1 & 2 Timothy, Titus, Philemon). Only then may we profit from all the other Scriptures, applying all that we find in them which harmonizes with the truth of our heavenly calling. Then we shall be mature men of God, completely furnished into every good work, (2Timothy 3:17).

Now the basis of all *Practical Christianity* is love, but we must never forget that:

"We love Him because He first loved us," (1 John 4:19).

And how deeply He loved us! He gave His only begotten Son, Who took upon Himself the likeness of sinful flesh in order to redeem us by His shameful death upon the cross at Calvary. Such is the love of God which He commends to us. While we were ungodly enemies, while we were yet sinners, Christ died for us! (Romans 5:6-10). Such love is the spring of our love to Him. Because He is love He embraces a world of sinners, not just us, and pours out His own love into our hearts by His Holy Spirit so that it may overflow to others also.

Our love to Him, which springs from His love to us, is the only acceptable motive for *Practical Christianity*. If that love is lacking then whatever we may do, however good it may look in our eyes or however great it may appear in the eyes of others, in God's sight it is nothing but empty formality.

Practical Christianity is our passing on His love to others. Thus it involves relationships towards God, member of Christ's Body, the family, people at work, the state, enemies and all mankind. What does the Bible teach us about these?

Our Relationship towards God

The whole purpose of our redemption is not merely to bring us into a state of salvation but is to bring us to Him – that He may be all in us as one day He will be all in all. We are a kind of first fruits.

All God's grace and blessing to us flows through His Son, Christ Jesus, in Whom we stand by faith but we are not only in Christ Jesus. We are in Christ Jesus our Lord. We belong to Him by virtue of the fact that we have been bought with a price, and what a price that was! He owns us. We belong to Him. Therefore, Paul's exhortations are but reasonable.

> Present yourselves unto God, as those that are alive form the dead, and your members as instruments of righteousness unto God. (Romans 6:13)

I beseech you therefore, brethren, by the mercies of God, that ye present your bodies a living sacrifice, holy, acceptable unto God, which is your reasonable service. (Romans 12:1)

These two verses just about summarize the practical side of our relationship to God. Notice, however, that Paul does not say in Romans 12:1,

"I command or order you to present your bodies."

It is as if he goes down on his knees and begs and implores us. It is by the mercies of God, and he has just written about these in the first eight chapters of his epistle. How like God! He never asks us to give Him anything without first giving us the enabling power to do it.

O that some modern evangelists would take this lesson to heart and cease preaching a gospel of surrender and start proclaiming the gospel of the grace of God. This, alone, gives both the motive and the power for a person to surrender, or rather present, himself to God.

In Romans 1:1 Paul calls himself "a servant of Christ Jesus" but the Greek word for servant is more correctly translated bond slave.

Perhaps Paul had in mind the Jubilee Year teaching given in the Old Testament. Then all slaves were released from the service of their masters and allowed to go their own way.

However, under this law there was a provision for the slave who said, "I love my master. I will not go free." Such a slave would then submit to having his ear pierced with an awl, which was the symbol of his acceptance of being a bond slave for life, (Exodus 21:2-6). Such was Paul's love for his Lord. Once the proud Pharisee but now the humble life-long bond slave of the One he formerly persecuted.

> I would not work my soul to save,
> For that my Lord hath done.
> But I would work like any slave

From love to God's dear Son.

So says a verse in an old hymn and perhaps it would be a good thing if each one of us pondered again in our hearts, our relationship towards God.

Our Relationship towards Members of the Body of Christ

There is one Body of Christ and only one, (Ephesians 4:4). God, alone, has chosen and placed each member in that Body and no man can put out any of them, yet divisions and excommunications abound.

Paul, in his letter to the Corinthians, severely rebukes them for making little bodies of their own. They were saying,

> "I am of Paul, yet I am of Apollos, yet I of Cephas, yet I of Christ," (1 Corinthians 1:12).

Today things are far worse than in Paul's time for, in spite of their divisions, the Corinthians did at least meet together in the same place, (1 Corinthians 11:20). Now, not only do we have a multiplicity of bodies – Anglicans and Catholics, Baptists and Brethren (closed and open), Pentecostal and Presbyterian etc. – but they all form separated communities and all meet in separate places. Today attempts are being made to unify the various groups by patching up their differences in doctrine and compromising their customs.

Such attempts at unification ignore the one unity that God has made, the spiritual unity of each individual member of the Body of Christ. Scattered among all the various denominations are individuals whom God has called and placed in the one spiritual Body of Christ. We do not have to make this unity. It has already been made. But we are told to:

> "keep the unity of the Spirit in the bond of peace," (Ephesians 4:3).

This is not easy to do and this may be why Paul tells us to endeavour to do so. It requires:

"humility, meekness and patience, bearing with one another in love," (Colossians 3:12-13).

Today we live in perilous times and the faith once delivered to the saints is being shipwrecked. Not so much from the outside world of unbelievers but from the inside, from those who profess and call themselves Christians – some of whom sit in high places. With whom, then, should we have fellowship? The divine answer is given to us in 2Timothy 2:22:

"Follow after righteousness, faith, love, peace, with all who call on the Lord out of a clean heart."

This effectually ignores the barriers which men have erected.

Of course, not all members of the one Body of Christ see eye to eye in the interpreting of Scriptures. There are different views. There are degrees of knowledge, and ignorance, but these should not be allowed to prevent us from having fellowship with each other. Let us base our fellowship on the life of a person, not merely on his doctrine. After all the Scriptures say,

"By their fruits ye shall know them," (Matthew 7:16, 20).

his is not to dismiss true doctrine as being of no account. It is vitally important as no one can become a member of Christ's body without believing at least the Gospel of God concerning His Son. There is no spiritual life apart from Christ.

However, it is noteworthy to see how Paul, in his first letter to the Corinthians, deals with a brother in Christ who has committed an immoral act. He is to be shunned! Paul even prays for his deliverance into the hand of Satan,

"for the destruction of the flesh, that the spirit may be saved in the day of our Lord Jesus."

In his second letter, it is evident that such drastic action had borne fruit unto repentance for Paul asks the church "to forgive him and comfort him," (1Corinthians 5:1-5; 2Corinthians 2:1-8).

Now there were some at Corinth who denied the resurrection of the dead – a vital doctrine for if this is so, then Christ is not raised and we are still in our sins! Did Paul kick them out of the church? No! He endeavoured to prove to them that if they were right, all his preaching was in vain, that they were still in their sins and that the dead in Christ were perished. Moreover, if in this life only they had hope in Christ, then they were of all men the most miserable, (1 Corinthians 15:12-19).

Is there not a great lesson for us to learn here? Immoral acts by fellow Christians require drastic action, even banishing – with a view to their repenting and then being forgiven and restored to fellowship. On the other hand, those who err in doctrine should not be excommunicated but patiently borne with – with a view to their acknowledgment of the truth in due time. Let those of us who think we are mature not be puffed up with pride because of the knowledge we have. Neither let us look down upon those we consider babies in Christ. Rather let the strong help the weak, remembering that the hall-mark of one who is mature is meekness, gentleness, patience, bearing with all and, above all, love. Let us not confine our fellowship to those with whom we agree but let us fellowship where we are permitted, "with all who call on the Lord out of a clean heart."

Our Relationship towards Members of our Family

It was in two of the epistles Paul wrote while in prison at Rome that he gave precepts to govern the lives of husbands, wives and children; (Ephesians 5:25-6:4; Colossians 3:18-24). Here we are given with a few strokes of the pen a graphic picture of the Christian family who are in the Lord. Where the lordship of Christ is acknowledged and where these precepts are obeyed, the blessedness of harmony and peace will ensue in that family.

From press, radio and television we read, hear and see divorce, family strife, broken homes, cruelty to children and many other sad and pitiful incidents. In vain do the psychiatrists, sociologists and well-meaning people attempt to remedy these disasters but the solution does not lie on the surface. Only as individual families come to know the Lord and respond to His gracious authority is there harmony and peace. In this wilderness of strife and violence which fills the world today, how blessed is the Christian home where the Lord is given His proper place as Head.

But let us consider the practical precepts mentioned in Ephesians and Colossians. First the husband and father.

Husbands are exhorted to love their wives and be not bitter towards them. Harshness of speech is a wounding thing to a wife and is the direct opposite of love. Love is kind and affectionate and its depth toward the wife is to be like the depth of love that our Lord shows to each individual member of His Body. How deep that love is!

No man hates his own flesh, and husband and wife are one flesh. So, too, are the members of Christ's body – in spirit. Would Christ ever sever one of His own members, however unworthy and unfaithful? No! So how can husbands contemplate divorcing their wives? They cannot if they are to love them as Christ loves the members of His Body. How truly great is this secret!

But what of fathers? It is their sacred duty to bring up their children in the discipline and admonition of the Lord. How gracious is that discipline and admonition! Behind them is a love which will not hesitate to use the rod when necessary, so how sickly and sentimental are the educationalists today who tell us that children should never be disciplined as it will repress them. We are now seeing some of the fruit of their labours in today's society and some of those poor children are appearing in the juvenile courts.

Fathers must not vex their children. Unfair punishments, insistence on punctilious obedience to unnecessary and niggling rules, sarcasm and biting comments will discourage children and make them rebellious. Let fathers, by their example and teaching, bring up their children in the discipline and admonition of the Lord.

Wives have but one precept; simply, "to be subject to their husbands as is fitting in the Lord," (Colossians 3:18). There is a tendency today to put some women on a pedestal. They are exalted, in many spheres which were once the prerogative of men, not only to a position of equality but to one of superiority. It is very true that women can do equally well, if not better, many things previously done by men alone, but with the feminist advance has come the overthrow of the divine intention that the wife should be subject to her husband. Unfortunately, in opposing the modern trend there are those who have reduced woman to nothing more than a servile creature who can have no mind or will of her own.

There is nothing degrading in an intelligent woman being subject to her own husband. In fact, this is a divine instinct and in a crisis many women instinctively turn to their husbands for help.

A true husband will always listen to the view and opinions of his wife and put many of them into practice. Many men lean on the wisdom of their wives, though perhaps they do not always admit it! When husbands are loving, tolerant, sympathetic and understanding with their wives and when wives are subject to their husbands, then there is perfect peace and harmony in the marriage.

Children, also, are given but one simple, yet far-reaching, precept:

> "Obey your parents in all things, for this is well pleasing in the Lord," (Colossians 3:20).

In the Old Testament the command to

> "honour thy father and mother" had the promise of "long life in the land" attached to it, (Exodus 20:12).

This, perhaps, shows the importance the Lord attached to it. Sadly, one of the prevalent signs of our times is the disobedience of children to parents, which we not only read and hear about but which we often see before our eyes.

Side by side with this goes the exaltation of children over adults, of the young over the aged. There is a tendency to give responsible positions to the young, long before they are ready to cope with them. Although young people develop more rapidly in knowledge these days, they do not necessarily have the wisdom for the big responsibilities which are thrust upon them so early in their lives.

Suffice it to say that the only precept given by the Lord to children is,

"Obey your parents in all things."

The son or daughter who is obedient displays humility which is the hall-mark of future exaltation, in both things of this world and in things spiritual.

Where husbands love their wives and are not bitter towards them; where wives are subject to their husbands; where fathers bring up their children in the discipline and admonition of the Lord and do not vex them; where children obey their parents – there is a family living in peace and harmony.

Our Relationship towards People at Work

I have chosen this headline to cover the believer's attitude towards work, both manual and clerical, and the relationship between the boss and the workers – the master and servants as the New Testament puts it.

When we come to think of it, for most of us the greater part of the day is spent being occupied in the ordinary, routine affairs of daily life. How we would like to get away from it all and devote more time to the study of God's Word and the ministry of it to others, but this is not possible.

In Paul's first epistle to the Thessalonians he had to rebuke certain zealous believers who were so obsessed with the work of the Lord and the apparent nearness of His return that they were neglecting their mundane, daily duties and, as a result, were becoming a burden on others, (2Thessalonians 3:10-12). There may be some believers like that today but Paul wrote that

> "if any provide not for his own, and especially for those of his own house, he hath denied the faith, and is worse than an infidel," (1Timothy 5:8).

A believer who does not provide for his family, a believer who slacks at his work and other duties is successfully undermining his testimony to unbelievers.

Now as to the relationship between the modern boss and worker, the precepts given by Paul concerning masters and servants are very applicable to today – see Ephesians 6:5-9 and Colossians 3:22-4:1. As believers we should obey those over us, with proper respect, with singleness of heart and as to Christ. It should not be with an outward show to please men but should be done cheerfully as to the Lord. This is not easy, especially when the boss is difficult to please, unfair and even harsh. But we are reminded that the Lord will compensate us with the enjoyment of the inheritance (Colossians 3:24-25) and that whatever good we may do will be rewarded to us by Him.

The same principle applies to the believing bosses as to the workers. They are reminded of their master in the heavens so they must be just and fair to all their workers, not given to threatening. We are living in days of strife and strike, lock-out and work-in, antagonism and dispute but no amount of arbitration or mew agreements between employers and employees well solve the problem. It is only here and there, where the believing boss and Christian worker put into practice the truth contained in Ephesians and Colossians, that there will be a harmony and peace which will make trades unions and shop stewards superfluous.

Our Relationship towards the State

The believer's seat of government, citizenship, commonwealth or realm is in the heavens from where he awaits a Saviour, the Lord Jesus Christ, to transform this body of humiliation into a body, like unto His (Christ's) body in glory, (Philippians 3:20,21). Some believers infer from this that they need not pay much attention to earthly governments and their laws. They reason that since Christ's future Millenial Kingdom on earth will be the only truly righteous government of this world, human governments have no jurisdiction over them. This accounts for all kinds of anti-political behaviour by certain Christians.

Paul clearly tells us what are the functions of all human governments.

> The powers that be are ordained of God. Therefore he that resists the power, resists the ordinance of God: and they that resist

shall receive to themselves judgment ... for this cause ... render therefore to all their dues: tribute to whom tribute is due; custom to whom custom is due; fear to whom fear; honour to whom honour. (Romans 13:1-7)

We can easily see from these verses the corresponding duties we owe to the Government and Civil Authorities of our day. A believer should be a most exemplary and law-abiding person, not merely to escape punishment, not merely for conscience sake but because government is an ordinance of God. Moreover, this obedience should be rendered to whatever form of government is in power, be it democracy or dictatorship, even communist or fascist.

The only time believers come into conflict with the powers that be is when any human government should forbid us to read our Bibles, pray and worship our God, substituting the State for God, (Daniel 3).

Soviet Russia has tried hard to suppress her people worshipping God but without success, in spite of the persecution of those who remained faithful.

In China the Christian faith was ruthlessly suppressed, at one time under the pain of death. I read of a Chinese school for girls that was raided. All the girls were assembled and told to step forward if they were Christians. One girl of sixteen years of age promptly did and was immediately shot! Is she not yet another to find a niche in the hero's gallery? (Hebrews 11).

However, today a much more liberal attitude towards Christians is being taken by many authorities but we know that there will come a time when the man of sin (antichrist) will be revealed, demanding to be worshipped as God by all, with the penalty of extermination for those who refuse, (2Thessalonians 2:4; Revelation 13:15).

But returning to a more mundane situation: should a believer vote? I believe the answer to this is,

"Render therefore unto Caesar the things that are Caesar's and unto God, the things that are God's," (Matthew 22:21).

Personally, I exercise my vote to elect what I consider to be the most stable and beneficial government that will enable us to live "a quiet and peaceable life in all godliness and honesty." But whatever government is elected, it needs our prayers to this end.

> For this is good and acceptable in the sight of God our Saviour, who will have all men to be saved and come to the knowledge of the truth. (1 Timothy 2:1-4)

Our Relationship towards our Enemies

Our Lord said,

> "Love your enemies, pray for them that curse you, do good to them that hate you, and pray for them that despitefully use you, and persecute you," (Matthew 5:44).

We will find this precept very hard to obey unless we ourselves remember that we were once enemies of God and, when His enemies, we were reconciled to God through the death of His Son, (Romans 5:10). How God loves His enemies!

However, He does remember that we are but frail and so we are exhorted as much as lieth in us to be at peace with all men, (Romans12:18). We are not to avenge ourselves for any wrong done to us, but rather give place to wrath – for vengeance belongs to God, (Romans 12:19; Deuteronomy 32:35).

> "Therefore, if thine enemy hunger, fced him; if he thirst, give him drink: for in so doing thou shalt heap coals of fire on his head," (Romans 12:20).

Is not the motive behind this to win over the enemy to the faith?

Our Relationship towards all Mankind

Our attitude towards mankind in general is to be motivated by the fact that in this dispensation of the Grace of God, He is reconciled to all and beseeches them to be reconciled to Him, (2Corinthians 5:19). In the coming dispensation, the reconciliation will be withdrawn and He will be a *Man of War* in the day of wrath, (Ephesians 5:6).

Furthermore, we know that every man is potentially a son of God and not only should our verbal preaching of the reconciliation reflect this, but so should our unspoken attitude towards all men. Let us show our love for all mankind and by our love, I do not mean a sentimental condoning of their sins.

> Let love be without hypocrisy, abhor that which is evil, cleave that which is good. (Romans 12:9)

God loves the sinner, but hates the sin.

Moreover, let us remember that we were once

> "foolish, disobedient, deceived, serving divers lusts and pleasures, living in malice and envy, hateful and hating one another," (Titus 3:3).

It was only when the kindness of God our Saviour appeared to us that we were saved, not by our works of righteousness, but according to His mercy. Thus we should be gentle, showing meekness to all men. (Titus 3:2-5).

Concluding remarks

I realize that what I have written is but the barest outline of what may be termed *Practical Christianity*. Many points have been left untouched.

Also, I realize that in writing for others, I am made conscious of my own shortcomings in the practical walk of faith. However, I can say, without hypocrisy, that it is the sincere desire of my heart that I might wal worthily of the calling wherewith I am called, (Ephesians 4:1). Your calling as well as mine.

May God grant us grace so to live, that it might be truly said of us:

> The saving grace of God, which has appeared to all men, has taught us, that denying ungodliness and worldly lusts, we should live, soberly, righteously and godly in this present age, looking for that blessed hope, even the manifestation of the glory of

our great God and Saviour, Jesus Christ, who gave Himself for us that He might redeem us from all iniquity and purify into Himself a people for His own possession, zealous of good works. (Titus 2:11-14)

More on Practical Christianity

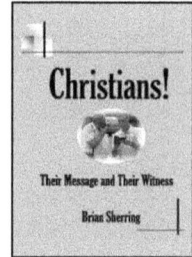

Christ's New Commandment
An examination of the biblical teaching on unity
Bryan Conway

Love! The greatest thing in the world
Henry Drummond

Love in the Bible
Michael Penny

Christians! Their Message and their Witness
Brian Sherring

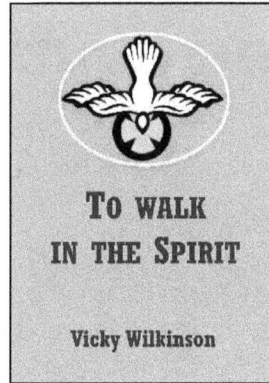

What Christians Believe and Do
By Vicky Wilkinson

To Walk in the Spirit
By Vicky Wilkinson

Further details of these books can be seen on
www.obt.org.uk

They can be obtains from that website and from

The Open Bible Trust
Fordland Mount, Upper Basildon,
Reading, RG8 8LU, UK.

They are also available as eBooks
from Amazon and Apple
and as KDP paperbacks from Amazon.

Free sample

For a free sample of
the Open Bible Trust's magazine *Search*,
please email

admin@obt.org.uk

or visit

www.obt.org.uk/search

About the author

James Poole was born in Finchley, London, in 1909 and took a course in Business Training at the City of London College. During his working years he was employed by various institutions and banks in the City of London. When he wrote this booklet he was enjoying retirement with his wife in Eastbourne, Sussex, but has since fallen asleep in Christ.

Also by James Poole

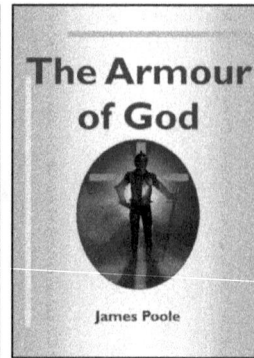

Abraham

James Poole

Isaac

James Poole

Jacob

James Poole

Joseph

James Poole

Notes on Ephesians

James Poole

The Armour of God

James Poole

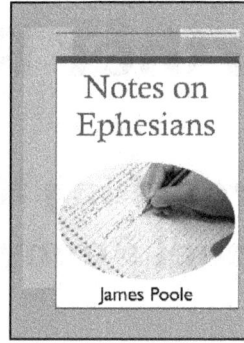

Further details of all the books here can be seen on **www.obt.org.uk**

The can be ordered from the website
and also from

The Open Bible Trust,
Fordland Mount, Upper Basildon,
Reading, RG8 8LU, UK.

They are also available as eBooks
from Amazon and Apple,
and also as KDP paperbacks from Amazon.

Further Reading

Approaching the Bible
Michael Penny

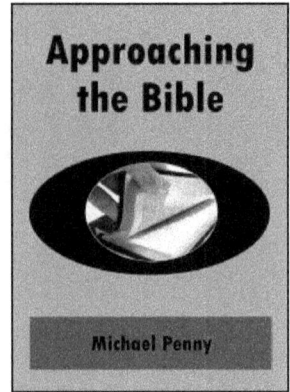

Approaching the Bible

Michael Penny

In easy to understand steps, and with many interesting examples, Michael Penny provides the rational for the view that before we try to *apply* any passage in the Bible to ourselves, we should discover first what it meant to those to whom its words were initially addressed. The book advocates that this is best done by considering the passage under the following headings:

1) **W**ho said or wrote it;
2) to **W**hom was it said or written, or concerning **W**hom was it said or written;
3) **W**here it was said or written, or concerning **W**here was it said or written;
4) **W**hat was said or written;
5) **W**hen was it said or written, or concerning **W**hen was it said or written;
6) **W**hy was it said or written.

Applying these six **"W"** rules puts the passage into its proper context and gives us the right perspective on it. Only after doing this can we determine:

7) **W**hether the passage applies to our situation and what the correct application is.

It is the *consistent* use of these **Seven Ws** which helps us discover the right and relevant application of any passage to our lives.

****

This book, and the one on the next page, can be ordered from **www.obt.org.uk** and from

The Open Bible Trust,
Fordland Mount, Upper Basildon,
Reading, RG8 8LU, UK.

40 Problem Passages
Michael Penny

This book is a sequel to *Approaching the Bible*.

The 7 Ws advocated in *Approaching the Bible* are applied to 40 difficult to understand passages. There are, of course, far more than 40 Problem Passages in the Bible. However, in this book Michael Penny not only solves these *40 Problem Passages*, but in doing so he equips the reader with a method by which many, many more hard to understand and difficult passages can be understood and successfully applied to the life of the believer today.

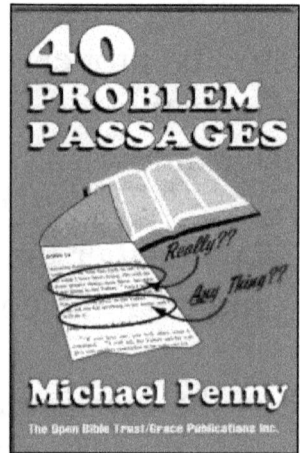

****

This book, and the ones on the previous pages, are also available as eBooks from Amazon and Apple,

and also as KDP paperbacks from Amazon.

About this book

Practical Christianity

"It is the divine purpose that faith is followed by works," writes James Poole and goes on to demonstrate the doctrine and practice cannot be separated. He considers what is practical for the Christian under the headings:

- Our relationship towards God
- Our relationship towards members of the Body of Christ
- Our relationship towards members of our family
- Our relationship towards people at work
- Our relationship towards the State
- Our relationship towards our enemies
- Our relationship towards all mankind

These seven relationships cover everything for the Christian who desires to please the Lord in his practical life.

www.ingramcontent.com/pod-product-compliance
Lightning Source LLC
Chambersburg PA
CBHW060610030426
42337CB00018B/3017